The Barking Lot
Animal Coloring Book for Kids

The Barking Lot
Animal Coloring Book for Kids

KF Wheatie & KM Wheatie

Strawberryhead &
Gingerbread Press

www.strawberryheadandgingerbread.com

The Barking Lot Animal Coloring Book for Kids

Published by Strawberryhead and Gingerbread Press
https://www.strawberryheadandgingerbread.com

Copyright © 2024 by KF Wheatie & KM Wheatie

All rights reserved. Neither this book, nor any parts within it may be sold or reproduced in any form or by any electronic or mechanical means, including information storage and retrieval systems, without permission in writing from the author. The only exception is by a reviewer, who may quote short excerpts in a review.

ISBN: 979-8-9906129-6-9 (paperback)

Lion

Lion

Lions are big cats known as the 'king of the jungle' with loud roars. They live in groups called prides and work together to hunt.

Giraffe

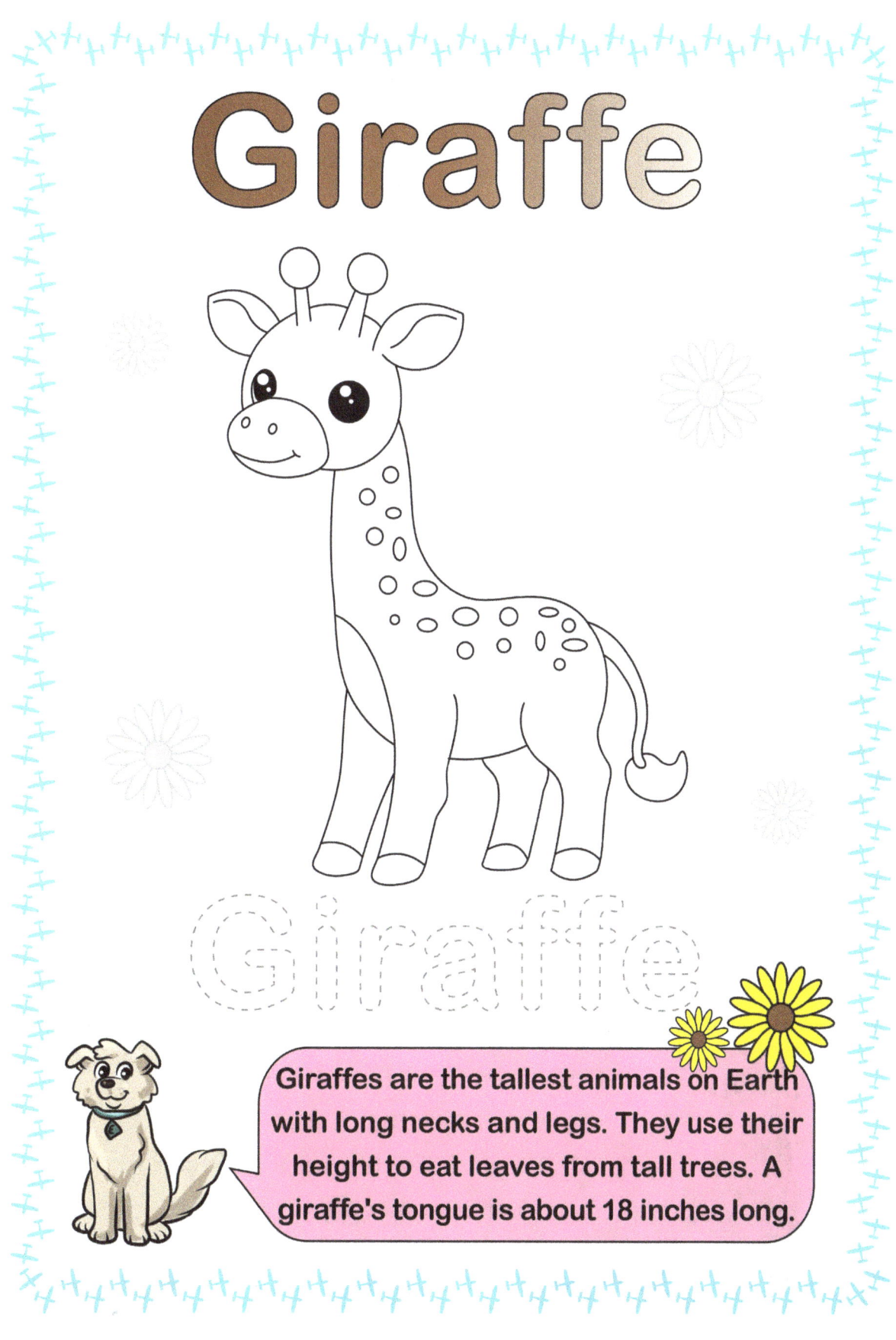

Giraffes are the tallest animals on Earth with long necks and legs. They use their height to eat leaves from tall trees. A giraffe's tongue is about 18 inches long.

Tiger

Tiger

Tigers are big and powerful cats. They are great swimmers and love to hunt in the wild. Each tiger's stripes are unique, like a fingerprint.

Monkey

Monkeys are playful & curious animals that love to swing through trees and eat fruits. They use their tails to help balance and swing around.

Zebra

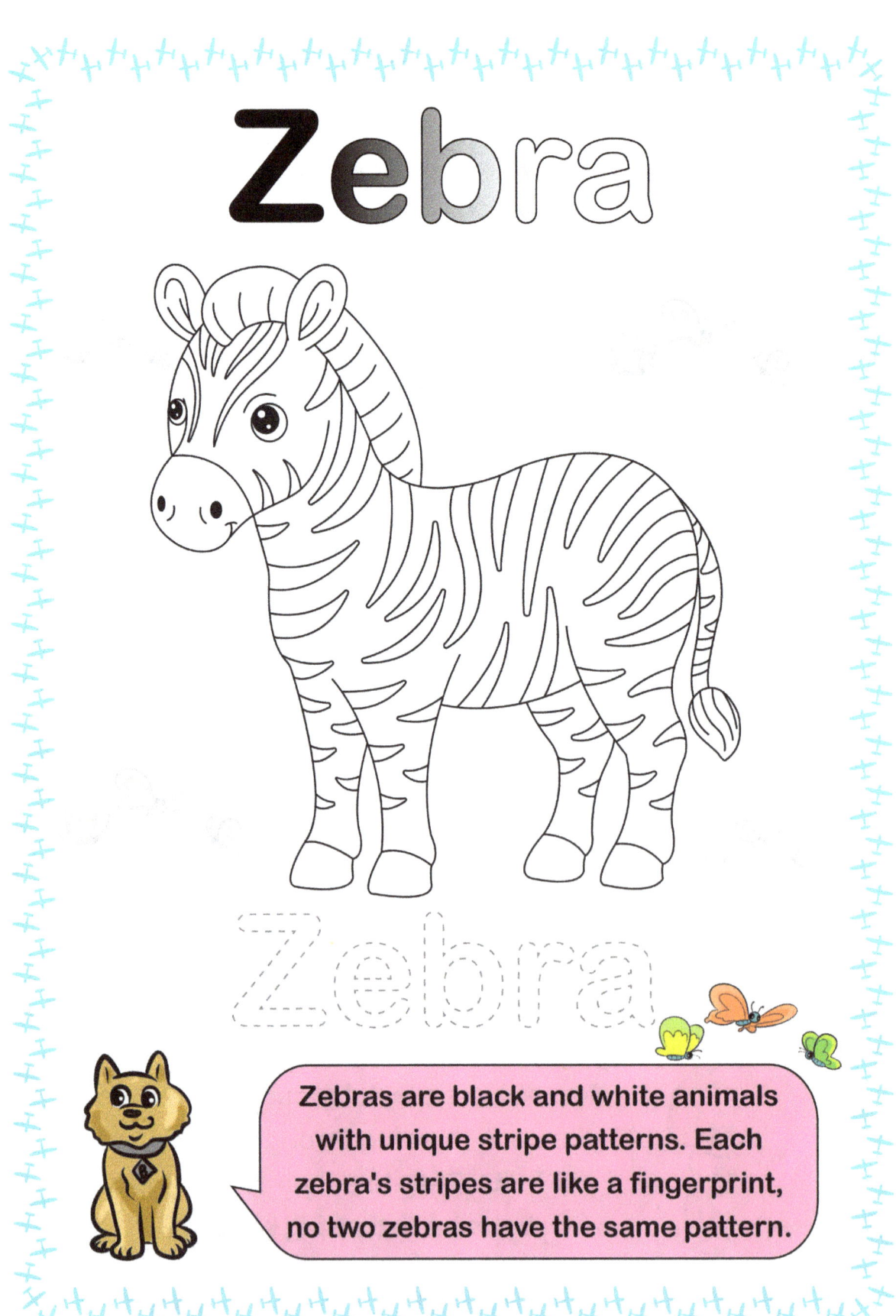

Zebras are black and white animals with unique stripe patterns. Each zebra's stripes are like a fingerprint, no two zebras have the same pattern.

Kangaroo

Kangaroos are large, hopping animals with strong legs and tails. They can leap up to 30 feet, and their tail helps them balance.

Panda

Panda

Pandas are cuddly bears with black and white fur that love to eat bamboo. Pandas spend about 12 hours a day eating bamboo to stay healthy.

Okapis

Okapis have zebra-like stripes on their legs and a giraffe-like body. They're called 'forest giraffes' because they live in Africa's rainforests.

Lemur

Lemurs are lively, tree-dwelling primates from Madagascar with long, fluffy tails. They use their tails to communicate with each other.

Chimpanzee

Chimpanzees are smart, social apes with expressive faces and strong arms. They can use tools, like sticks, to help find food in the wild.

Jaguar

Jaguar

Jaguars are powerful big cats with golden fur and black spots. Jaguars have the strongest bite of any big cat, strong enough to crush bones.

Squirrel

Squirrels are small, quick animals with bushy tails that love to climb trees. Squirrels can jump up to 10 times their body length to reach food.

Rabbit

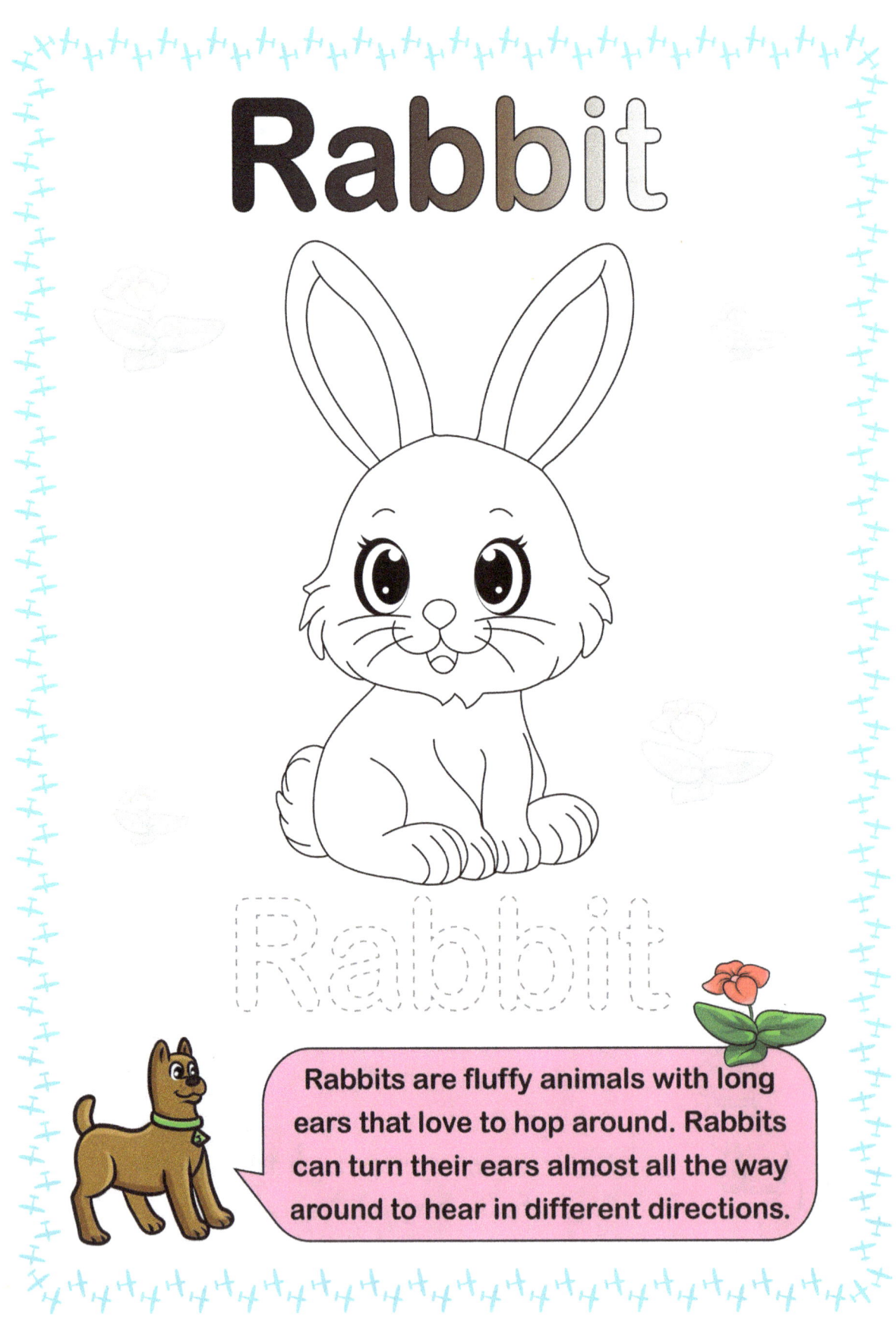

Rabbit

Rabbits are fluffy animals with long ears that love to hop around. Rabbits can turn their ears almost all the way around to hear in different directions.

Fox

Foxes are clever animals with sharp hearing that can detect sounds underground. Foxes can make over 40 different sounds to communicate.

Raccoon

Raccoons are curious animals with black 'masks' around their eyes and nimble paws. Raccoons can open jars and doors with their clever hands.

Bear

Bears are large, strong animals with thick fur and powerful claws. Bears can run very fast & are excellent swimmers, often covering miles in the water.

Wolf

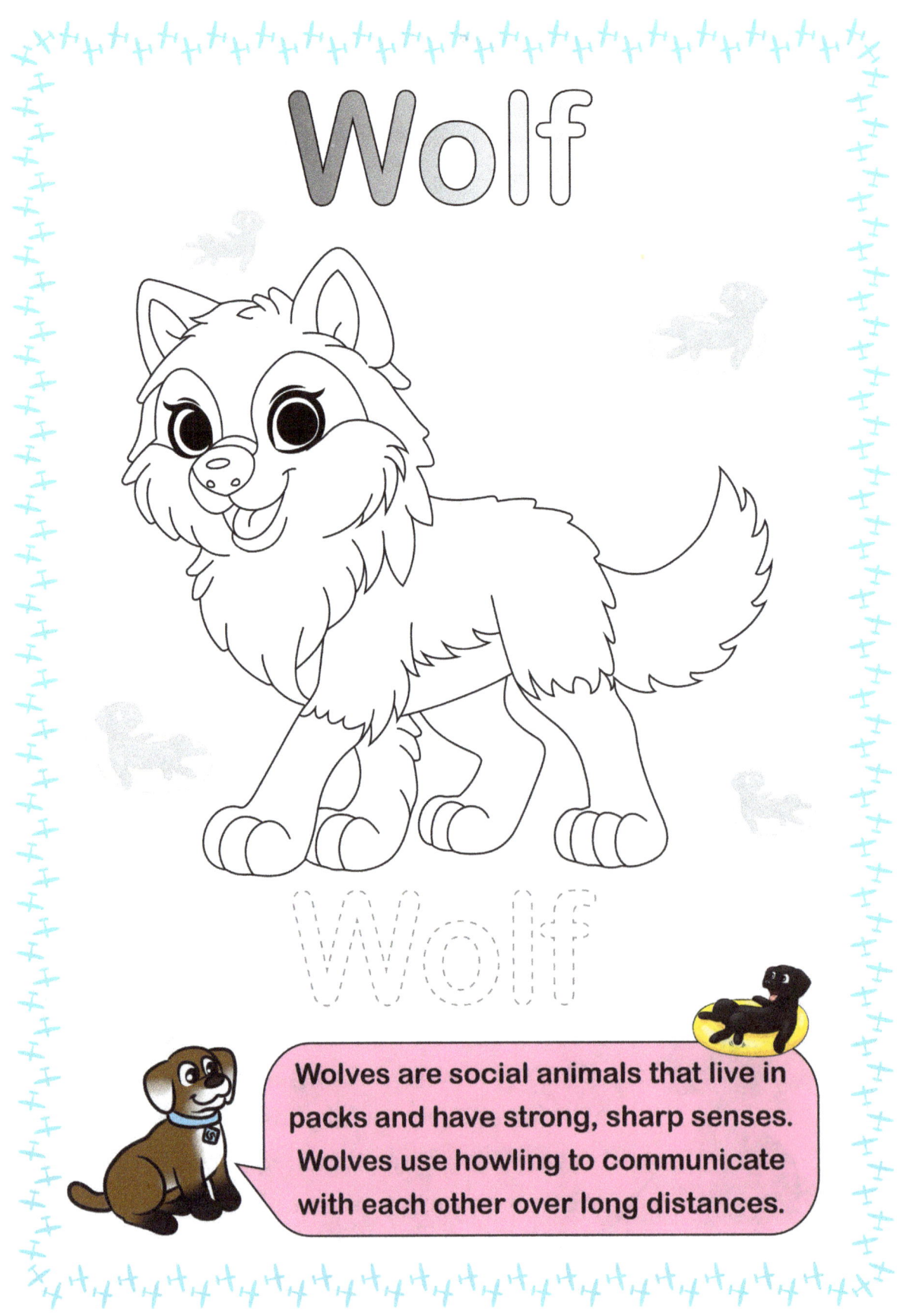

Wolf

Wolves are social animals that live in packs and have strong, sharp senses. Wolves use howling to communicate with each other over long distances.

Deer

Deer

Deer are specialized herbivores. Male deer are called bucks, stags while females are known as does or hinds. Deer can move their lips to grab leaves.

Koala

Koala

Koalas are tree-dwelling marsupials with fuzzy ears and a large nose. Koalas sleep up to 20 hours a day to conserve energy for eating eucalyptus leaves.

Rhino

Rhinos are large, thick-skinned animals one or two horns on their noses. Rhinos can weigh as much as 2,300 pounds & use their horns to defend themselves.

Hippo

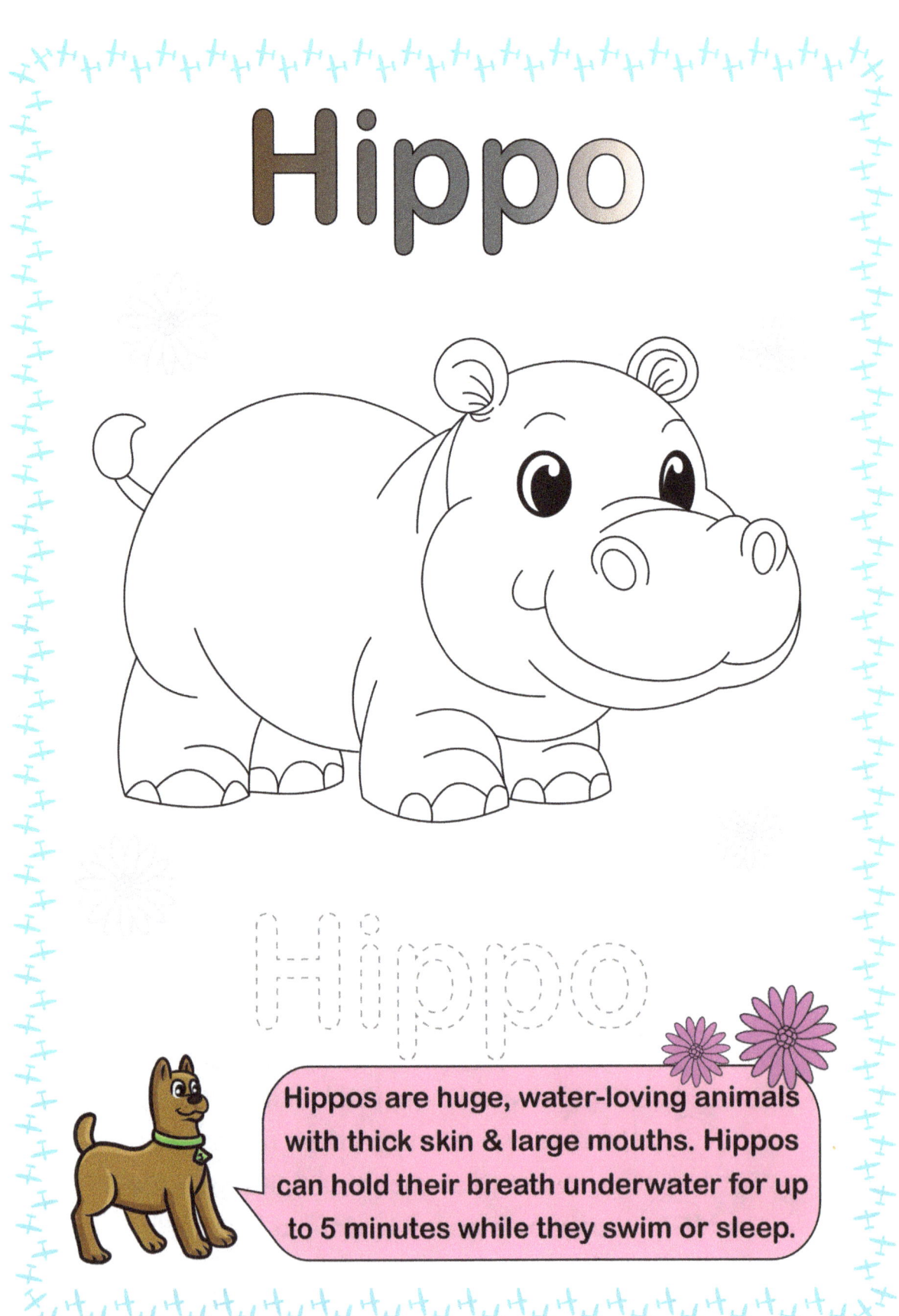

Hippo

Hippos are huge, water-loving animals with thick skin & large mouths. Hippos can hold their breath underwater for up to 5 minutes while they swim or sleep.

Donkey

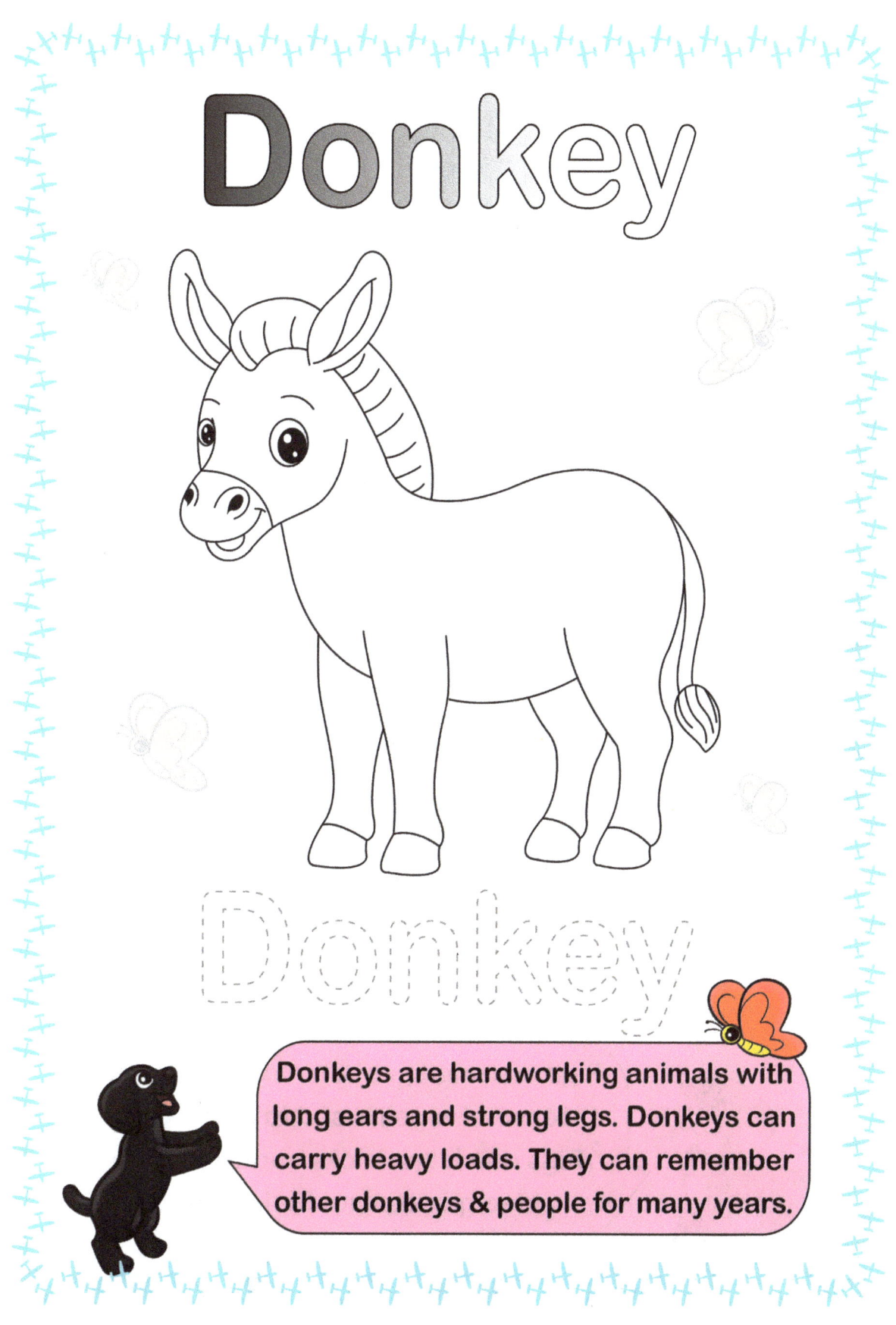

Donkey

Donkeys are hardworking animals with long ears and strong legs. Donkeys can carry heavy loads. They can remember other donkeys & people for many years.

Pig

Pig

Pigs are intelligent animals with great sense of smell, used to find food. Pigs can learn tricks and even play video games with their snouts.

Sheep

Sheep have thick woolly coats that they shed each year. They can recognize and remember faces of other sheep and people for years.

Goat

Goats have been used for milk, meat and fur. Goats have a special digestive system with four stomachs to break down tough plants.

Sheep have thick woolly coats that they shed each year. They can recognize and remember faces of other sheep and people for years.

Goat

Goat

Goats have been used for milk, meat and fur. Goats have a special digestive system with four stomachs to break down tough plants.

Cow

Cows are kept as livestock animals & are raised for their meat, milk & leather. They spend about 8 hours a day chewing their food to help digest it properly.

Meerkat

Meerkat

Meerkats are small, social mammals that live in groups called mobs. They take turns standing guard to watch for predators while others search for food.

www.ingramcontent.com/pod-product-compliance
Lightning Source LLC
Chambersburg PA
CBHW080535030426
42337CB00023B/4751